'93

merry christmas
Courtney!
love, Kelly

Other NEW YORKER Cartoon Books

The New Yorker Book of Cat Cartoons

The New Yorker Book of Dog Cartoons

The New Yorker Book of Doctor Cartoons

THE
NEW YORKER
BOOK OF LAWYER CARTOONS

THE
NEW YORKER
BOOK OF LAWYER CARTOONS

ALFRED A. KNOPF ✦ NEW YORK 1993

THIS IS A BORZOI BOOK
PUBLISHED BY ALFRED A. KNOPF, INC.

ISBN 0-679-43068-7
LC 93-61389

Manufactured in the United States of America

First Edition

THE
NEW YORKER
BOOK OF LAWYER CARTOONS

"I consider myself a passionate man, but, of course, a lawyer first."

"*Does <u>this</u>, by any chance, refresh your memory, Mr. Fillgate?*"

"Attention, please. At 8:45 A.M. on Tuesday, July 29, 2008, you are all scheduled to take the New York State bar exam."

"Your Honor, my client now realizes that his actions in the Unotek buyout and his transfers of funds to Swiss bank accounts were dreadfully immature."

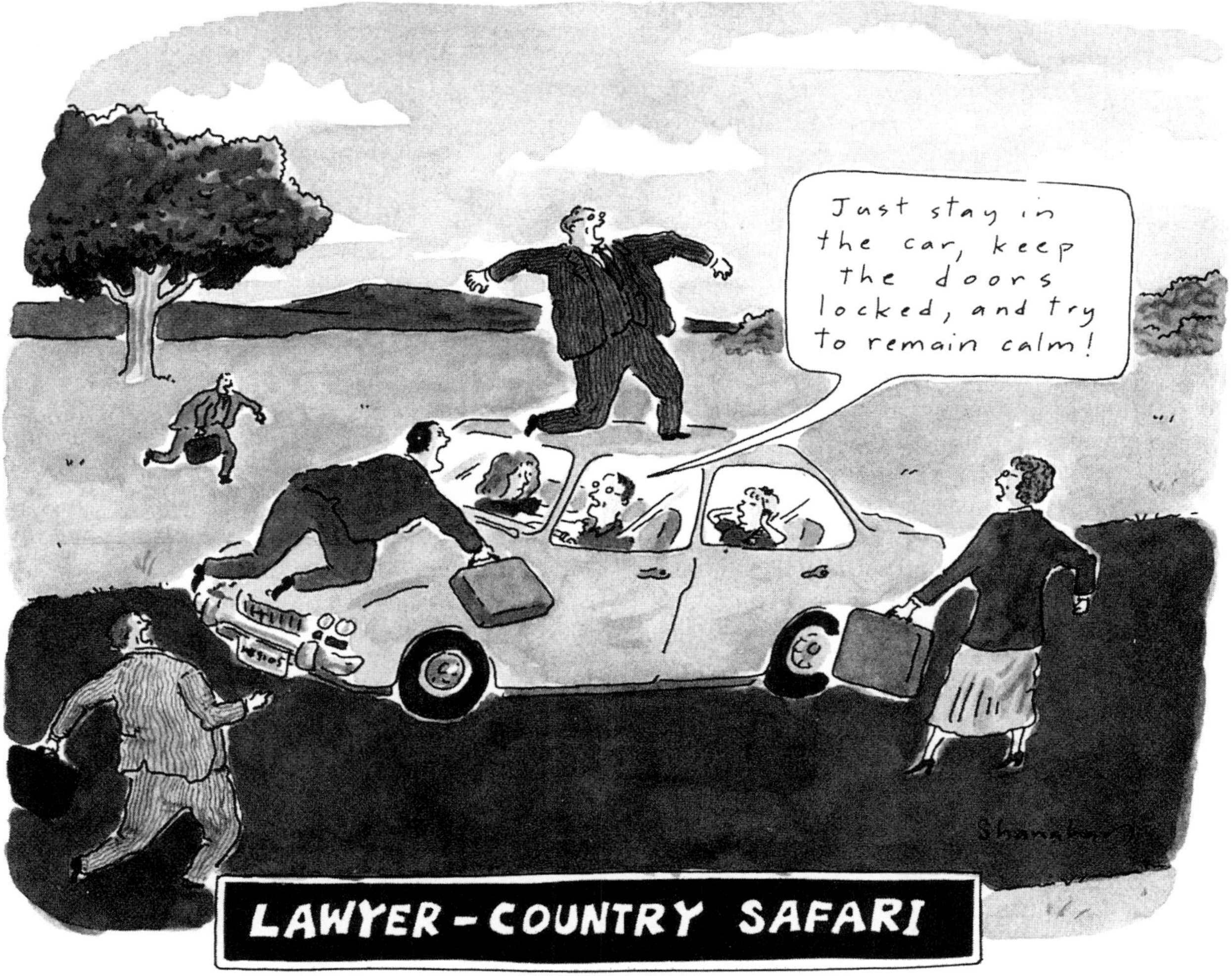
Just stay in the car, keep the doors locked, and try to remain calm!
Shanahan
LAWYER-COUNTRY SAFARI

"Damn it, when I say 'Opposing counsels may approach
the bench' I don't want high jinks!"

"Mac makes a great thing out of these reconciliations."

"*Your Honor, I object to the tactics of Lattimore, Finchley,*
Wilburn & Hatch!"

"I've just about resigned myself to your getting twenty years."

EVERYDAY HISTRIONICS
Weighing all the pros and cons

"Won't you please welcome Edwin Nells—accompanied,
as always, by his attorney."

"*I love you, Sharon, and these documents will advise you of certain rights you have in accordance with federal and state law, as well as variances and privileges you retain in the City of New York.*"

"Ladies and gentlemen, is there a bankruptcy attorney on board?"

"*Before we go on, could I speak to opposing counsel in my chambers?*"

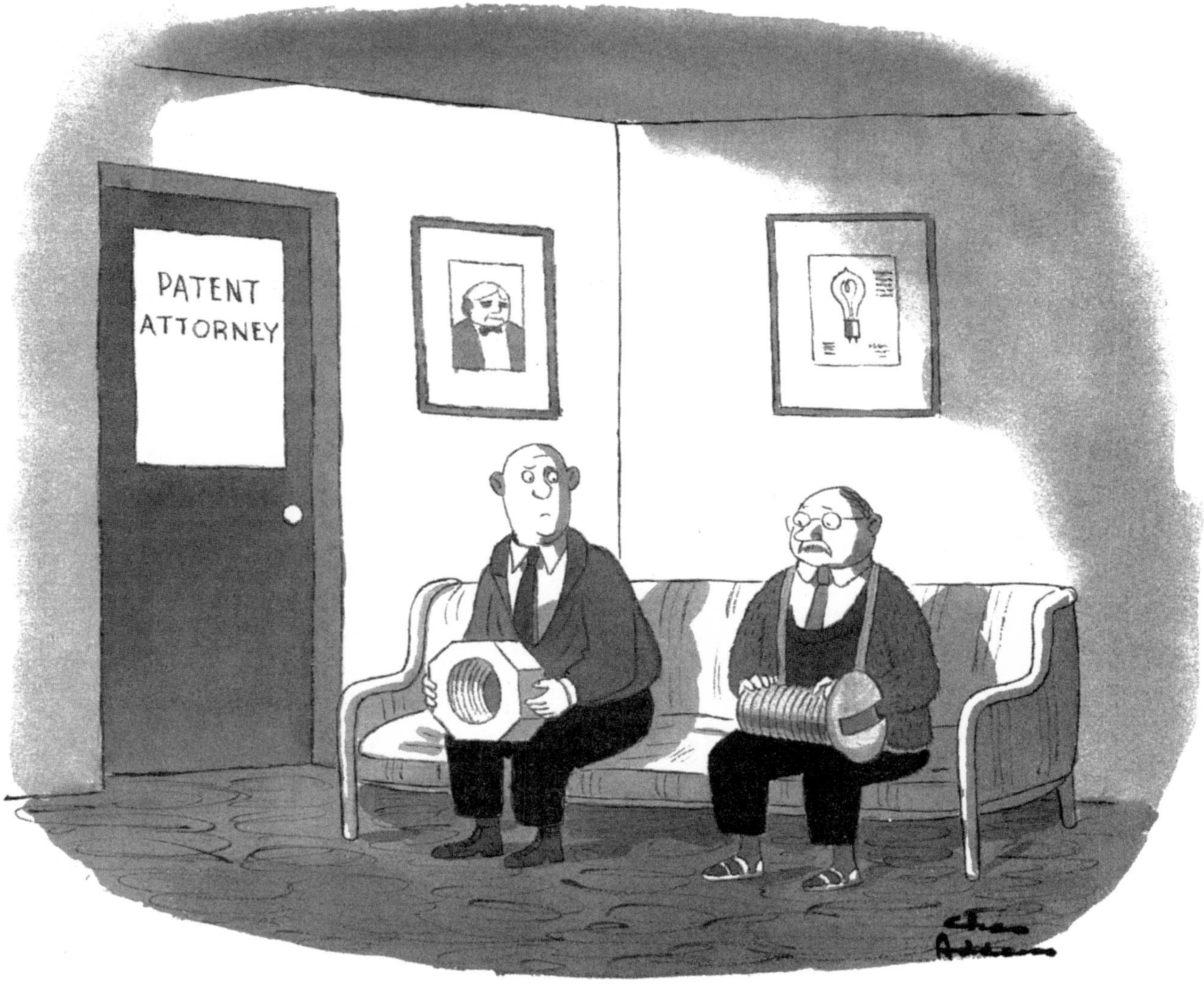
PATENT
ATTORNEY

"A unique and stirring plea, counsellor."

"I *am* a member of the legal profession, but I'm not a
lawyer in the pejorative sense."

"Now, now, Ruffy, if you'll spare me the threats
I'll spare you the legal jargon."

"May I ask you, Miss Howre, what made you select
a homeopathic attorney?"

"*I think going to law school helped my painting.*"

"'Ignorance of the law is no excuse.' Golly! I never heard _that_ one! Did _you_ ever hear _that_ one?"

KING ARTHUR AND THE ATTORNEYS OF THE ROUND TABLE

"Counsellor, please advise your client that, issues of personal
safety aside, gravity *is* the law."

"Hey, you two, pay attention, please! I happen to be trying to sway you!"

"Two lone corporate lawyers sitting down to do battle. Don't you find something rather thrilling about that?"

"See my attorney!"

"I'm speaking to you now not as man's best
friend but as your attorney's dog."

"Let me through. I'm a lawyer."

"*Do you know Kimberly, my attorney?*"

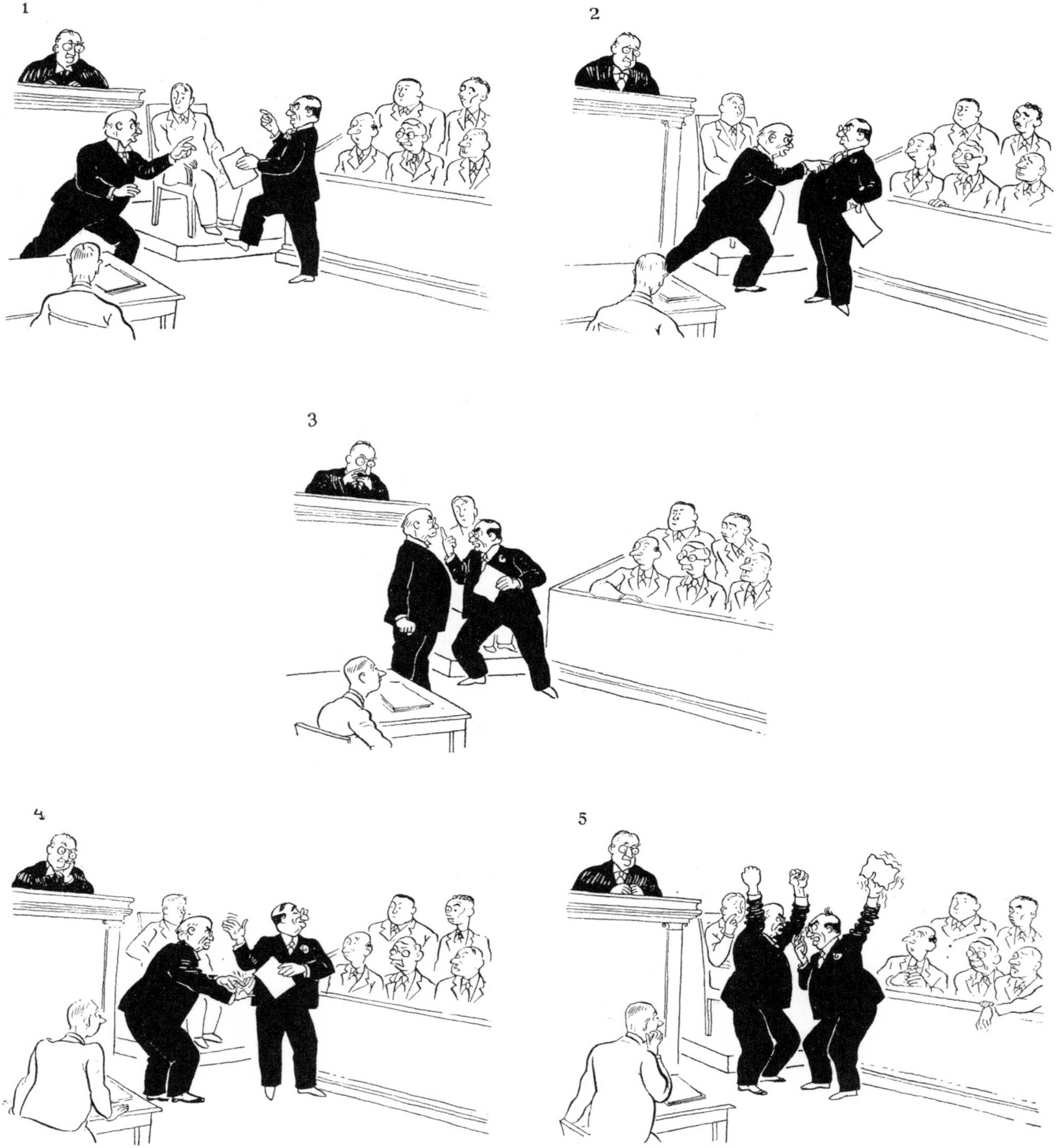
1
2
3
4
5

"The Court will take a recess until two p.m."

CARL ROSE

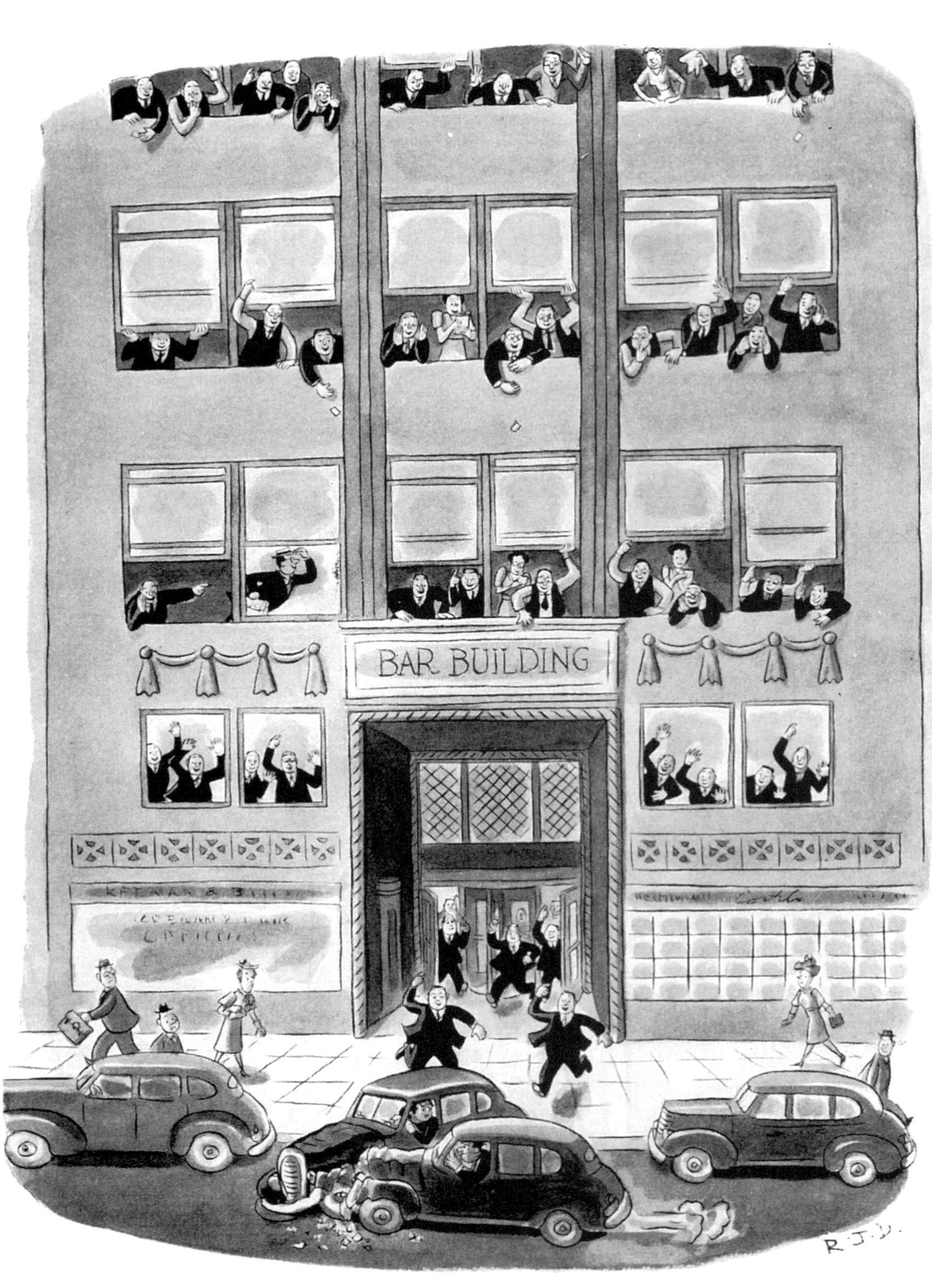
BAR BUILDING
R.J.D.

Opting for Chinese food for lunch, the law partners decide in principle to share their dishes and, accordingly, before ordering, negotiate a comprehensive pre-victual agreement.

NIGHT OF THE LIVING WILL

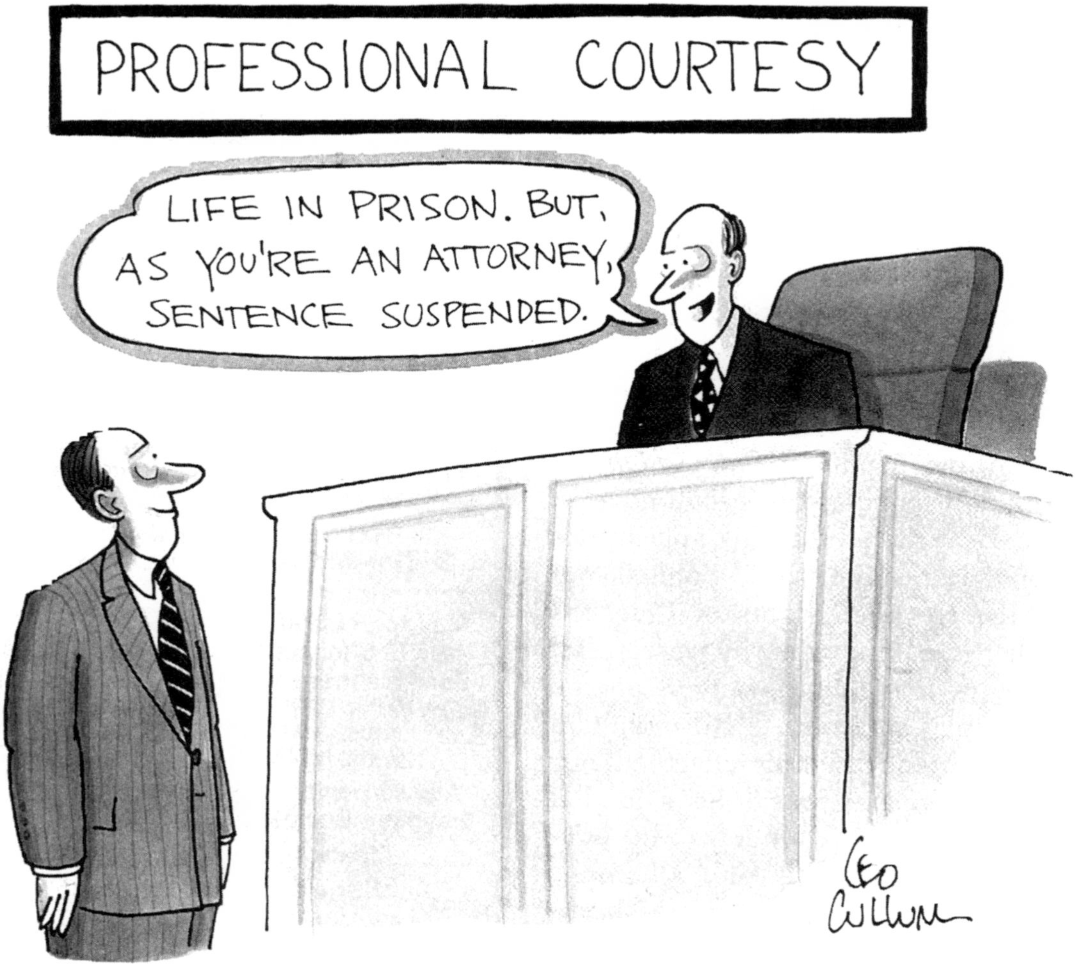
PROFESSIONAL COURTESY
LIFE IN PRISON. BUT, AS YOU'RE AN ATTORNEY, SENTENCE SUSPENDED.
LEO CULLUM

"Ladies and gentlemen, if after due consideration you find the balance of
the evidence to be against my client, I still beg of you to look into your
hearts and find compassion and mercy, because a verdict of guilty would make
this the tenth straight case I've lost in a row."

"*What better way to express your feelings about that certain someone's suit than to slap him with a massive countersuit?*"

"What do you do?"   "I'm a lawyer."
"The law."
"I do law."
"I practice law."
"I'm an attorney."
"Something legal."

"Look who's legal talent now!"

"I don't mind your acting as your own attorney, but would you please stop hopping on and off that damned chair?"

"*How very exciting! I have never before met a <u>Second</u> Amendment lawyer.*"

"Not <u>another</u> change of venue, counsellor!"

"Come now, Mr. Hillman, _everybody_ can't have a happy ending."

"*Ladies and gentlemen of the jury, say hi to my client.*"

"I'd like to present Mr. Bilkins. Mr. Bilkins is not a lawyer."

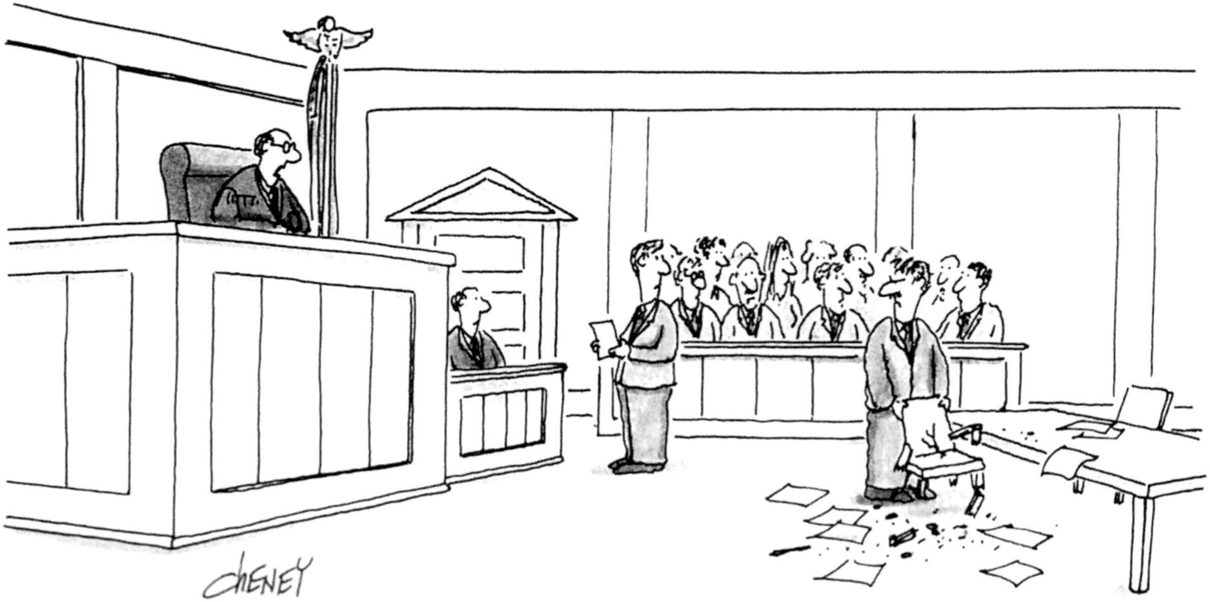
CHENEY

"Objection sustained."

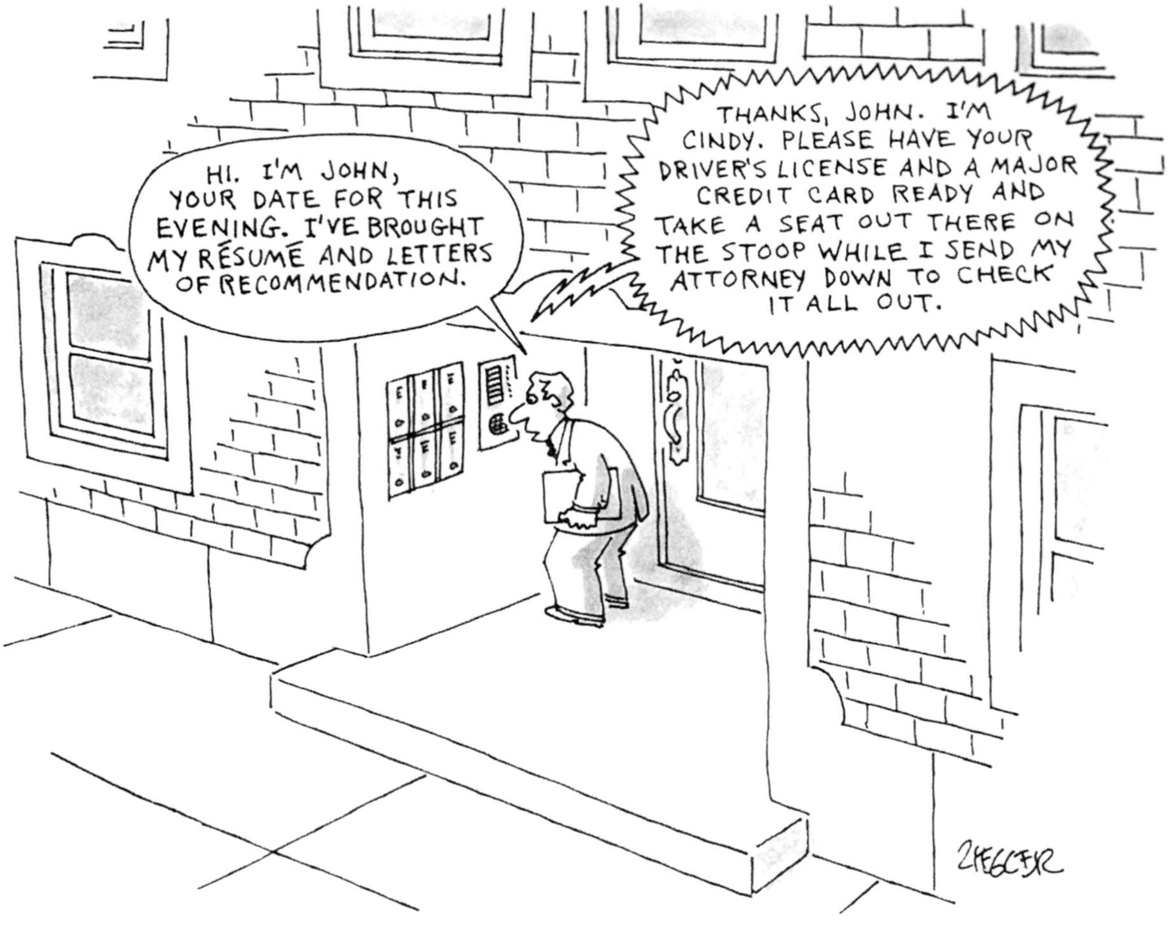
HI. I'M JOHN, YOUR DATE FOR THIS EVENING. I'VE BROUGHT MY RÉSUMÉ AND LETTERS OF RECOMMENDATION.
THANKS, JOHN. I'M CINDY. PLEASE HAVE YOUR DRIVER'S LICENSE AND A MAJOR CREDIT CARD READY AND TAKE A SEAT OUT THERE ON THE STOOP WHILE I SEND MY ATTORNEY DOWN TO CHECK IT ALL OUT.
ZIEGLER

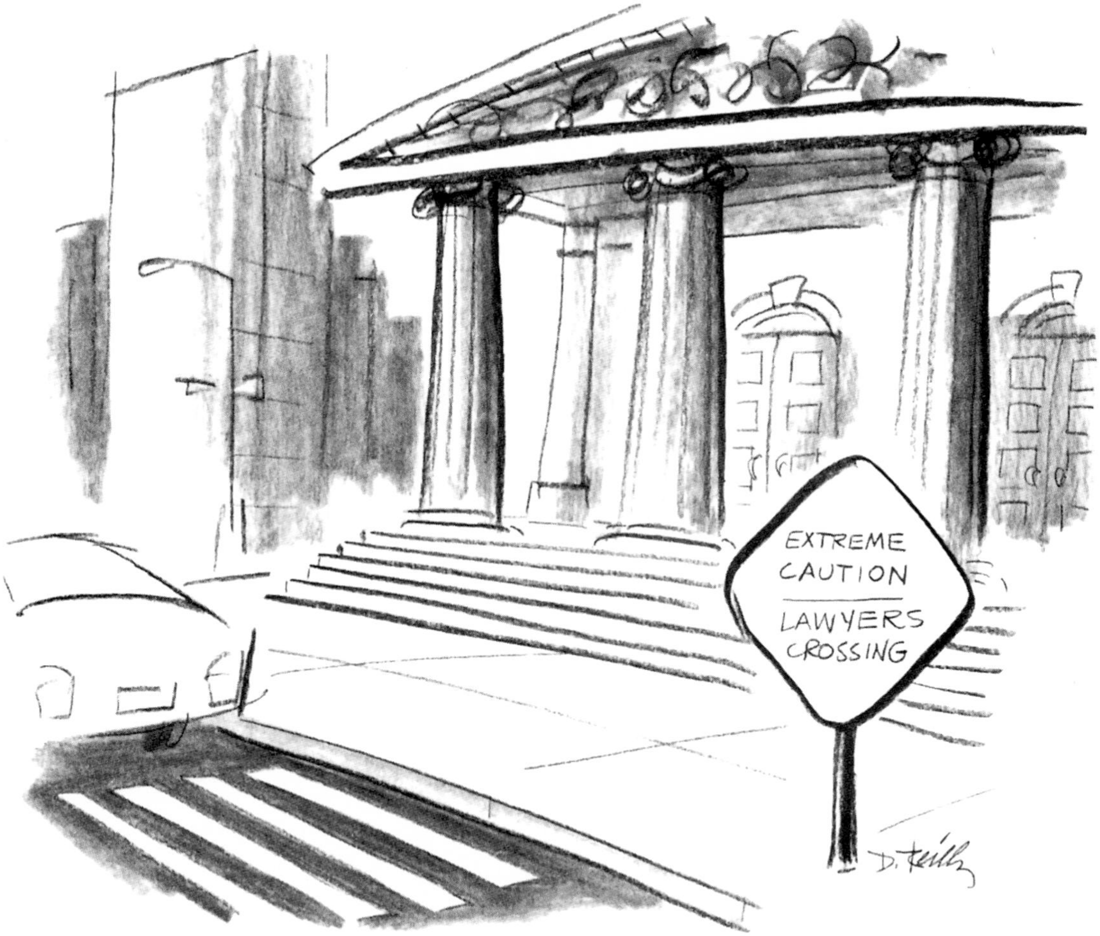
EXTREME
CAUTION
LAWYERS
CROSSING
D. Reilly

"It looks as if Fuller, McConochie & Vogel has opted for the dense-pack defense."

"*Look at it this way, Conroy—the longer they stay out,
the longer you're a free man.*"

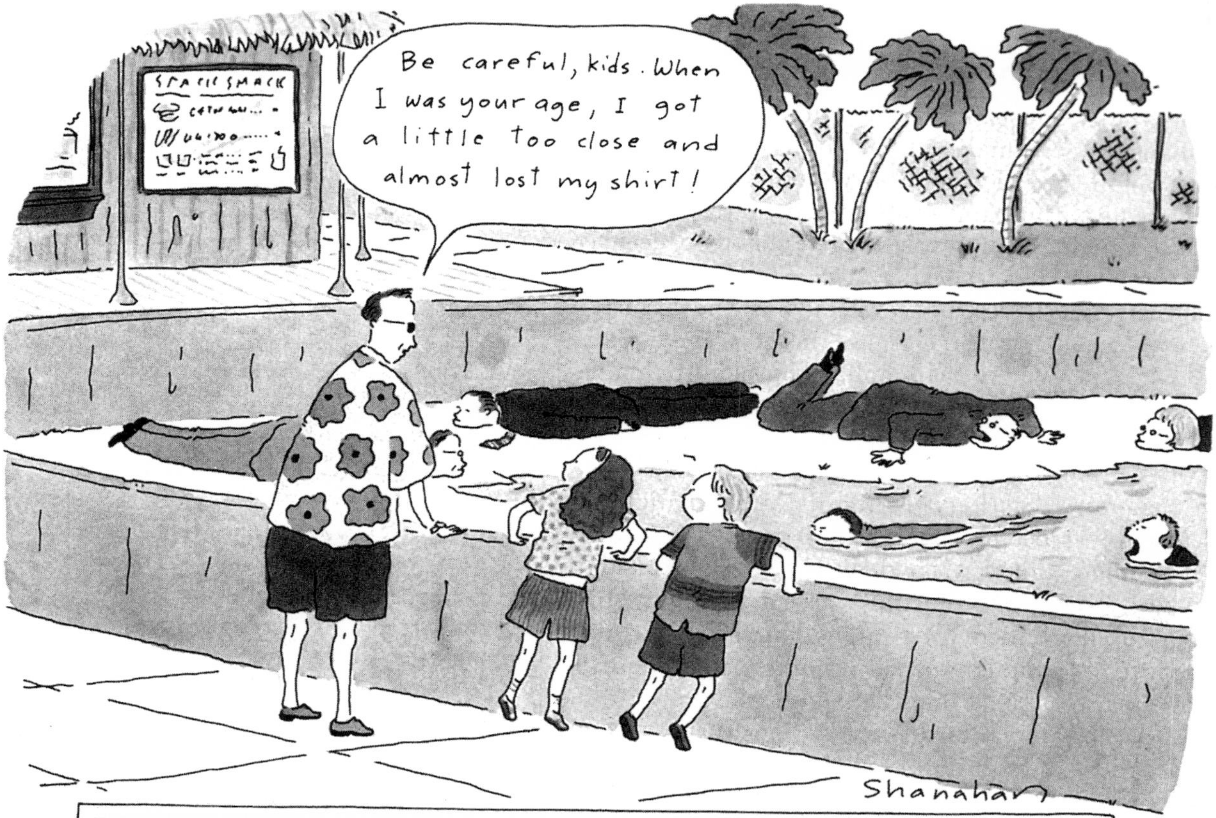
Be careful, kids. When I was your age, I got a little too close and almost lost my shirt!
Shanahan

UNCLE BERNIE'S LITIGATOR FARM

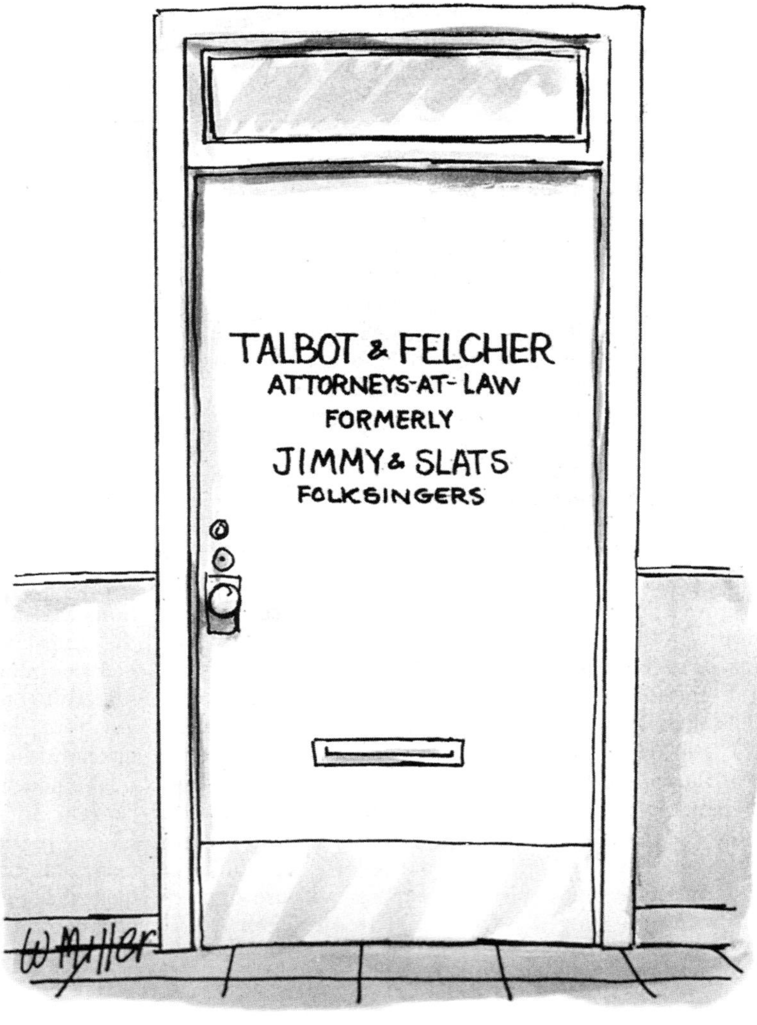
TALBOT & FELCHER
ATTORNEYS-AT-LAW
FORMERLY
JIMMY & SLATS
FOLKSINGERS
W Miller

"He's a brilliant attorney, but he can't stand to lose a case."

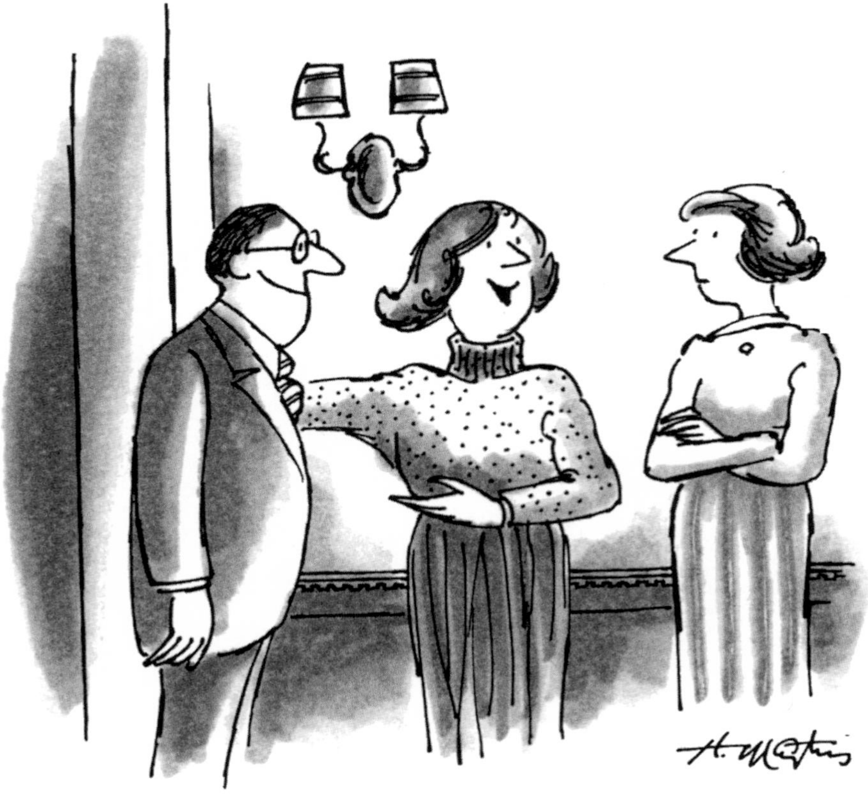
H. Martin

"Edna, this is Frank, my happiness, solace, delight, inspiration, comfort, joy, and lawyer."

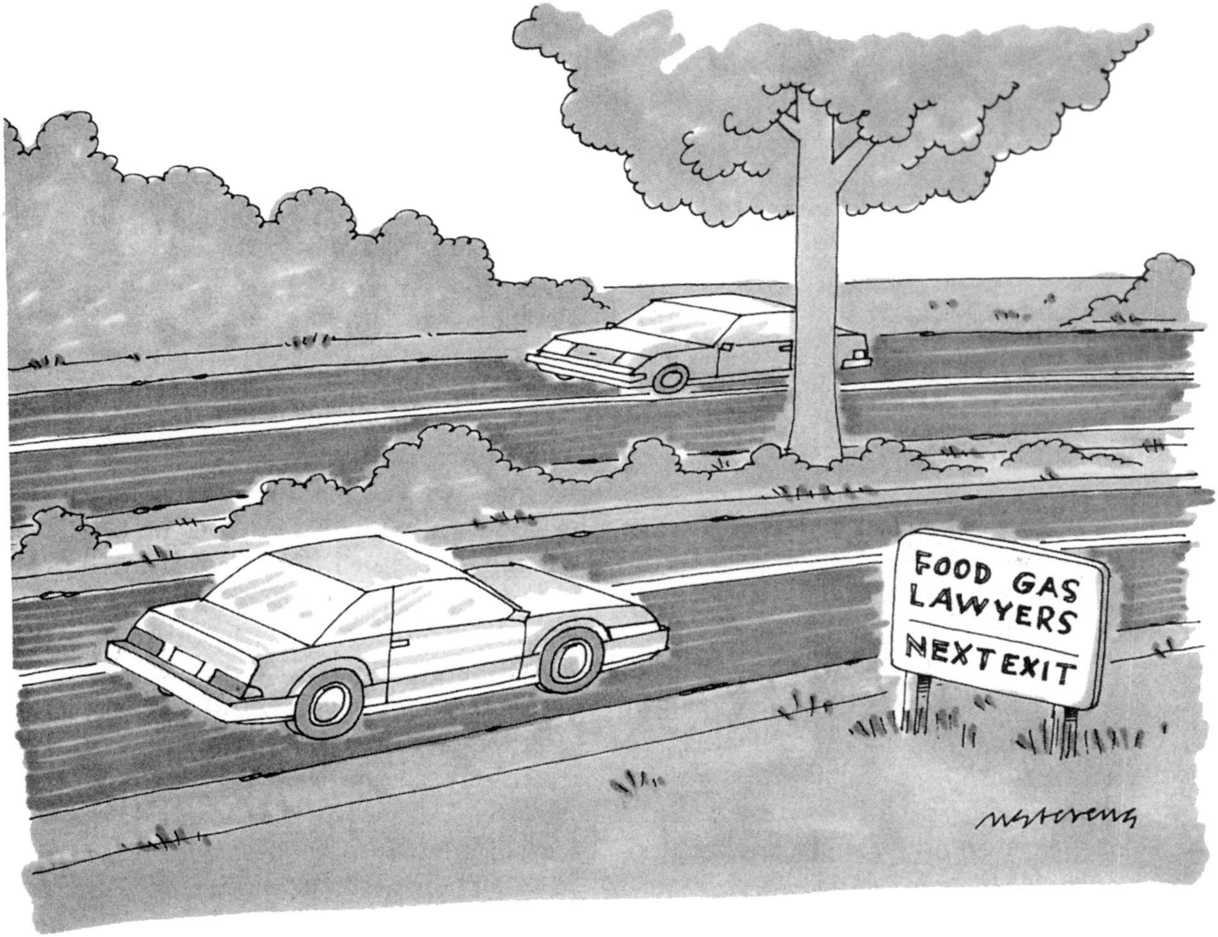
FOOD GAS
LAWYERS
NEXT EXIT

*"And then it hit me. I've reached that stage in life
where most of my friends are lawyers."*

"*I'm not quite ready to order. My lawyers are still studying the menu.*"

"*My client is sorry for what he did, and throws himself on the mercy of the Court.*"

"It's lawyerly, all right. But it's not legal."

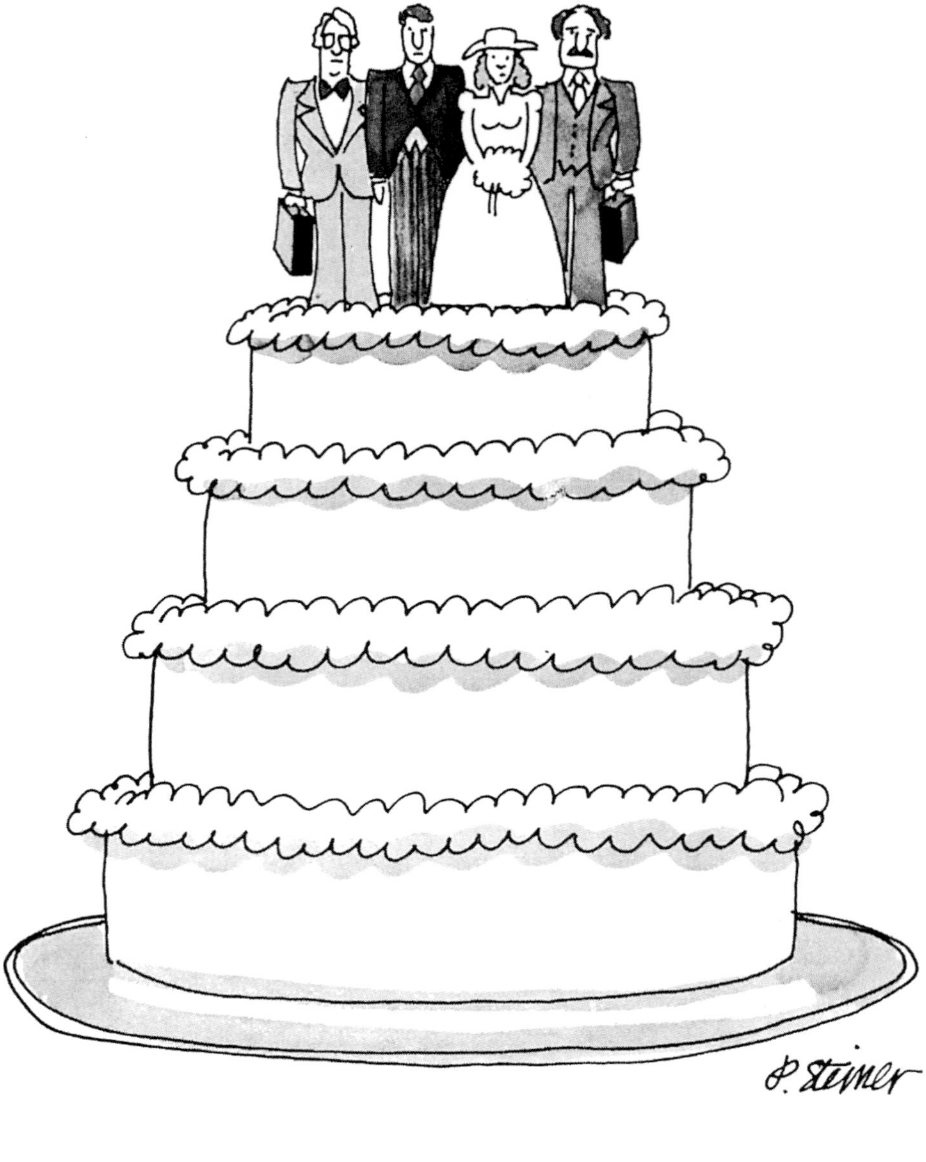
P. Steiner

"Look, I'm not saying it's going to be today. But someday—someday—
you guys will be happy that you've taken along a lawyer."

"*James J. Harris, attorney at law. My card, sir,*
in case you're overtaken."

"*Ed's a lawyer slash actor, Ron's a lawyer slash filmmaker, and Beverly's a lawyer slash playwright.*"

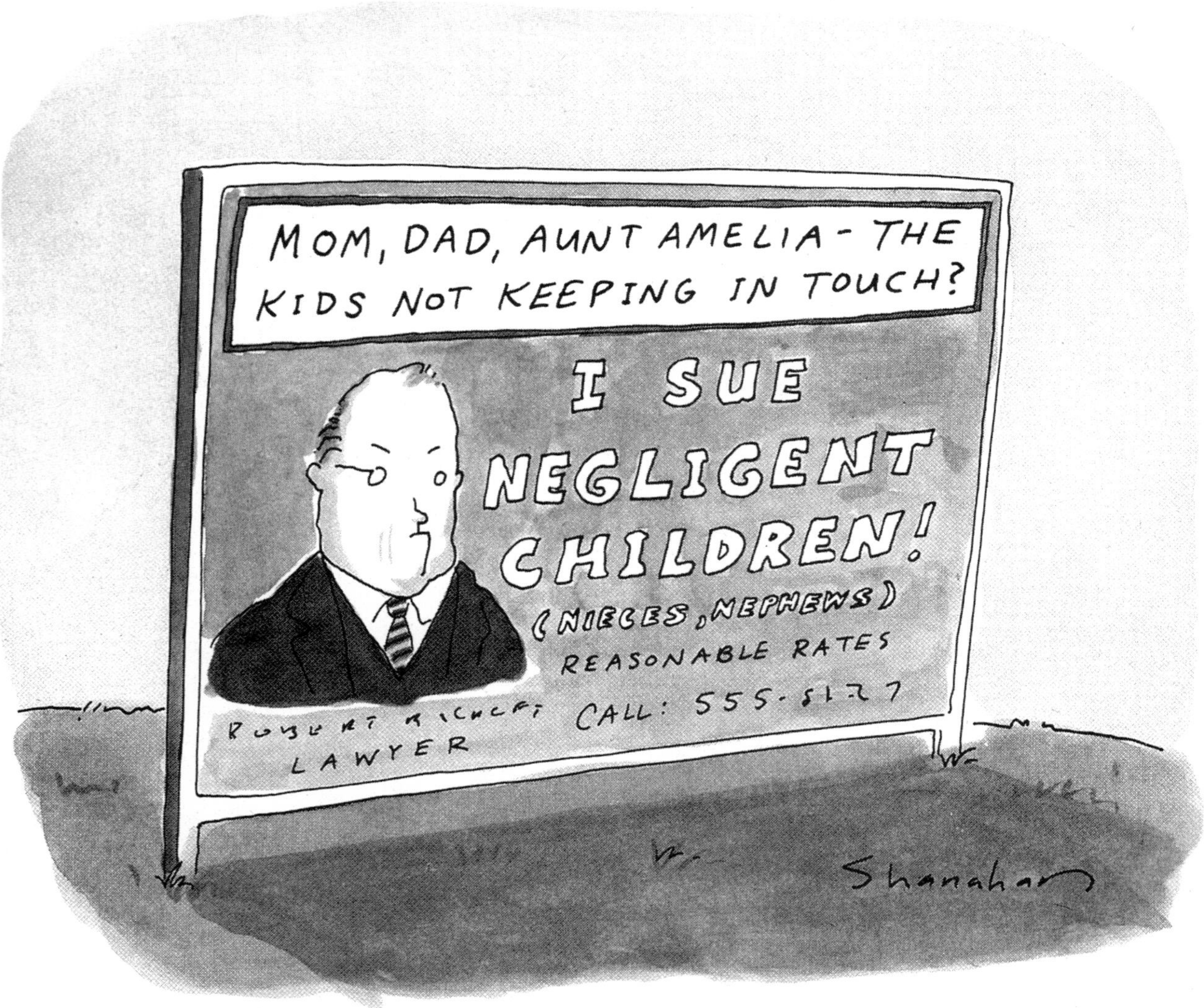
MOM, DAD, AUNT AMELIA - THE KIDS NOT KEEPING IN TOUCH?
I SUE NEGLIGENT CHILDREN!
(NIECES, NEPHEWS)
REASONABLE RATES
CALL: 555-
LAWYER
Shanahan

"Of course we could always enter a plea of insanity."

"I wish I had walls as thick as this in my apartment."

"*Don't get cute with me, counsellor.*"

ATTORNEY SIX-PACK

"As part of the settlement, your wife is asking for any three
of the six letters of your surname. You, of course, would retain
the remaining three."

"*What burns me up is that the answer is right here somewhere,*
staring us in the face."

"What is it this time? My maleness? My Anglo-Saxoness?
My Princetoness? My lawyerness?"

"He has his law degree and a small furnished office. It's just a
question now of getting him out of bed."

"*You have a pretty good case, Mr. Pitkin. How much justice can you afford?*"

"To answer your question. Yes, if you shoot an arrow into the air and it falls to earth you know not where, you could be liable for any damage it may cause."

*"You must realize, Your Honor, that my client is laboring
under a great mental strain."*

"Walter J. Hartley! Well, how do you like that for a coincidence? He was my lawyer, too."

"Ed, this is Art Simbley over at Hollis, Bingham,
Cotter & Krone. What did you get for thirty-four
across, 'Persian fairy,' four letters?"

"*The law, Williamson, is a jealous mistress, and that's something wives just have to understand.*"

*"Let me tell you, folks—I've been around long enough
to develop an instinct for these things, and my client is
innocent or I'm very much mistaken."*

"*Interesting. Have your lawyer call my lawyer.*"

"Never mind. I'm a lawyer myself."

"The ones just out of law school are especially frolicsome."

"That my client has been irresistible
to many women, I will be the first to admit."

"*And should you retain us, Mr. Hodal, you'll find
that we're more than just a law firm.*"

"*Would everyone check to see they have an attorney? I seem to have ended up with two.*"

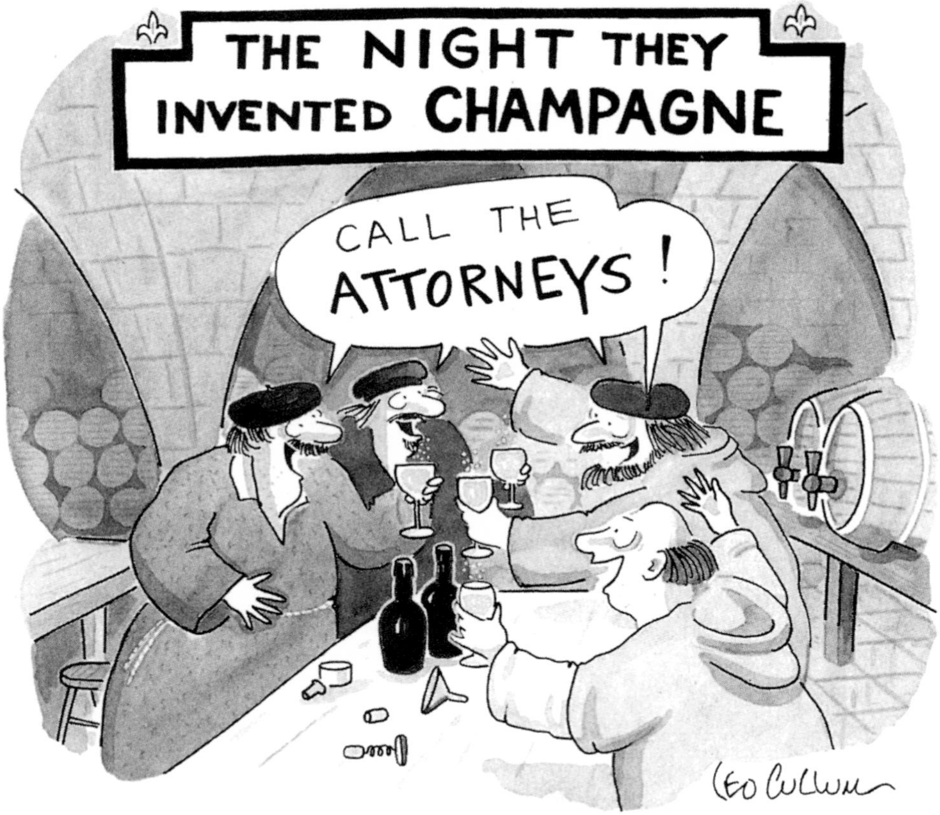
THE NIGHT THEY INVENTED CHAMPAGNE
CALL THE ATTORNEYS!

Index of Artists

The text of this book was set in a postscript version of Caslon Old Face No. 2 on a Macintosh. Printed and bound by Arcata Graphics/Martinsburg, Martinsburg, West Virginia
Designed by Virginia Tan